A+ books

How to Be
RESPONSIBLE

A Question and Answer
Book About Responsibility

by Emily James

CAPSTONE PRESS
a capstone imprint

Responsibility is a big word. But we all show responsibility every day.

Being responsible means doing the things you are supposed to do.

Sometimes being responsible means doing things you don't want to do.

There are lots of ways to show you are responsible.

Carter and his brother broke a lamp while playing.

His brother wants to lie about what happened.

What should Carter do to show he's responsible?

Carter tells his mom the truth. Being truthful shows responsibility.

Have you ever had to choose between telling the truth and lying?

Lily's bedroom is a mess!

What should Lily do to show she's responsible?

Lily cleans her room without being asked. Picking up after yourself shows responsibility.

Do you keep your room clean?

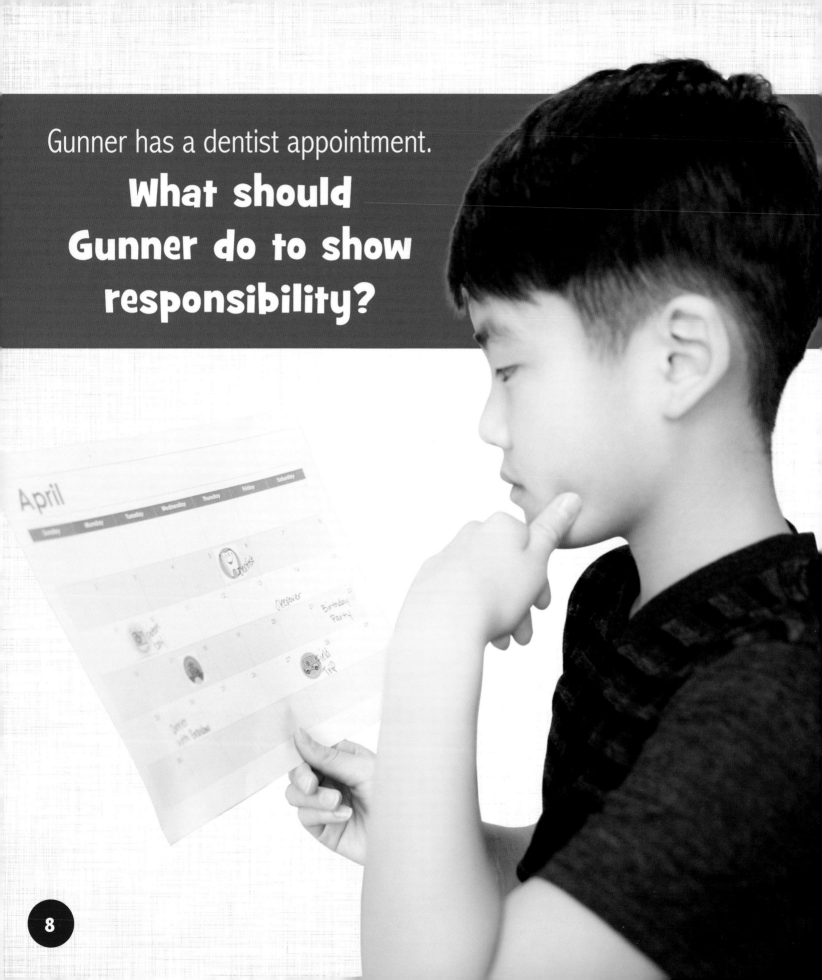

Gunner has a dentist appointment.

What should Gunner do to show responsibility?

8

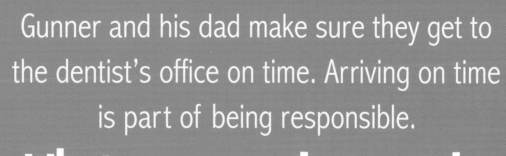

Gunner and his dad make sure they get to the dentist's office on time. Arriving on time is part of being responsible. **What can you do to make sure you arrive on time for appointments?**

Sofia just got a new puppy.

What should Sofia do to show she's responsible?

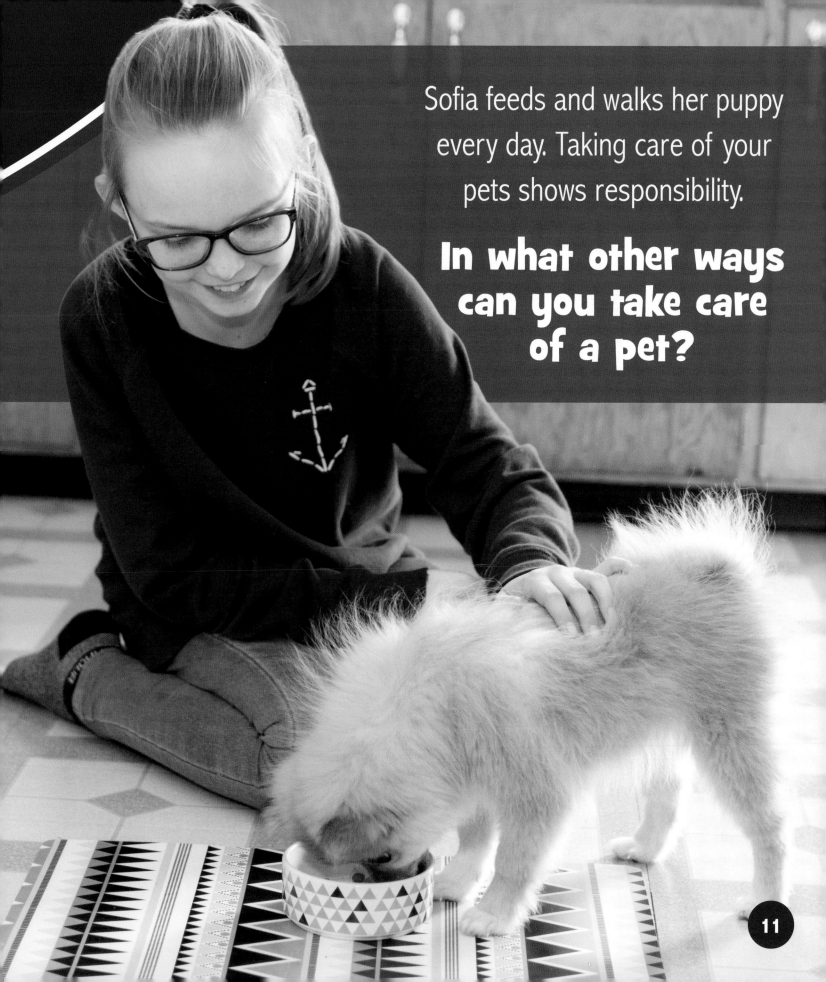

Sofia feeds and walks her puppy every day. Taking care of your pets shows responsibility.

In what other ways can you take care of a pet?

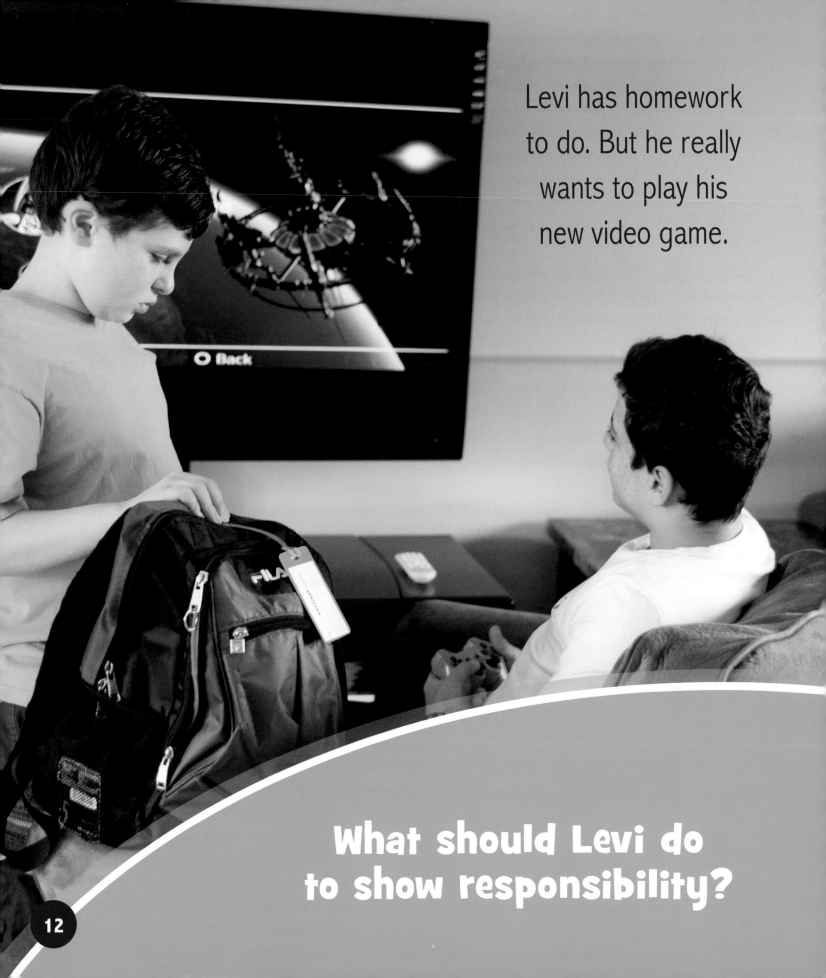

Levi has homework to do. But he really wants to play his new video game.

What should Levi do to show responsibility?

Levi does his homework.
Finishing your homework
first shows responsibility.

Do you do your homework before playing?

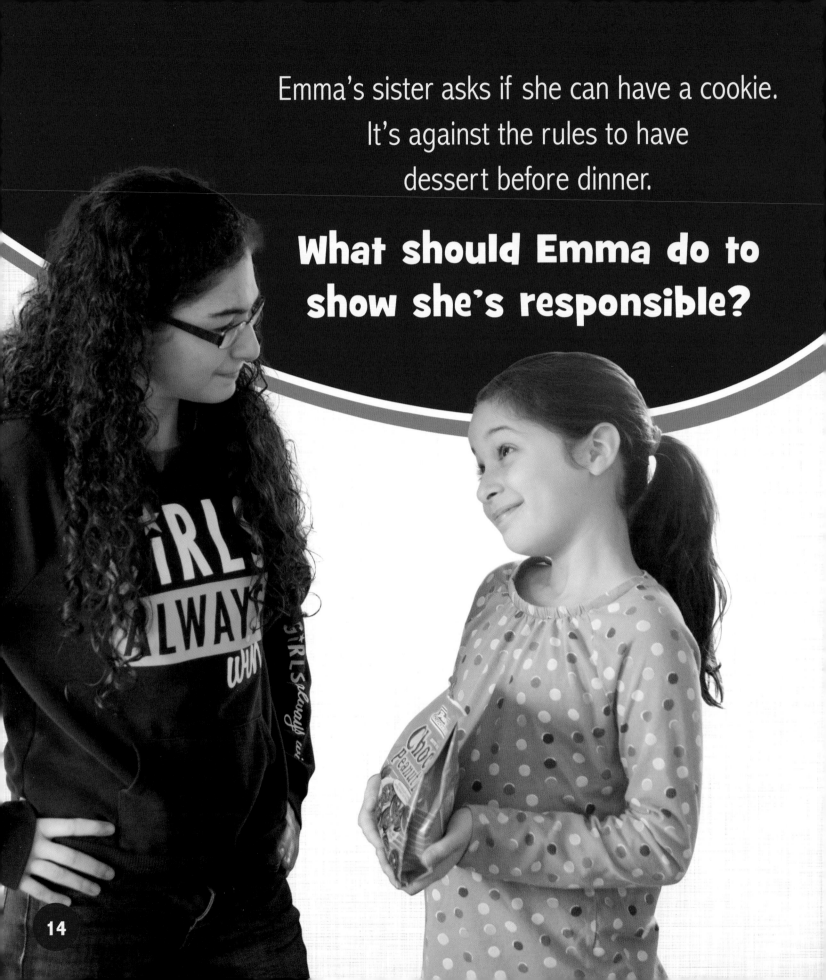

Emma's sister asks if she can have a cookie. It's against the rules to have dessert before dinner.

What should Emma do to show she's responsible?

Emma tells her sister no. Following the rules shows responsibility. **Has anyone ever asked you to break the rules?**

What did you do?

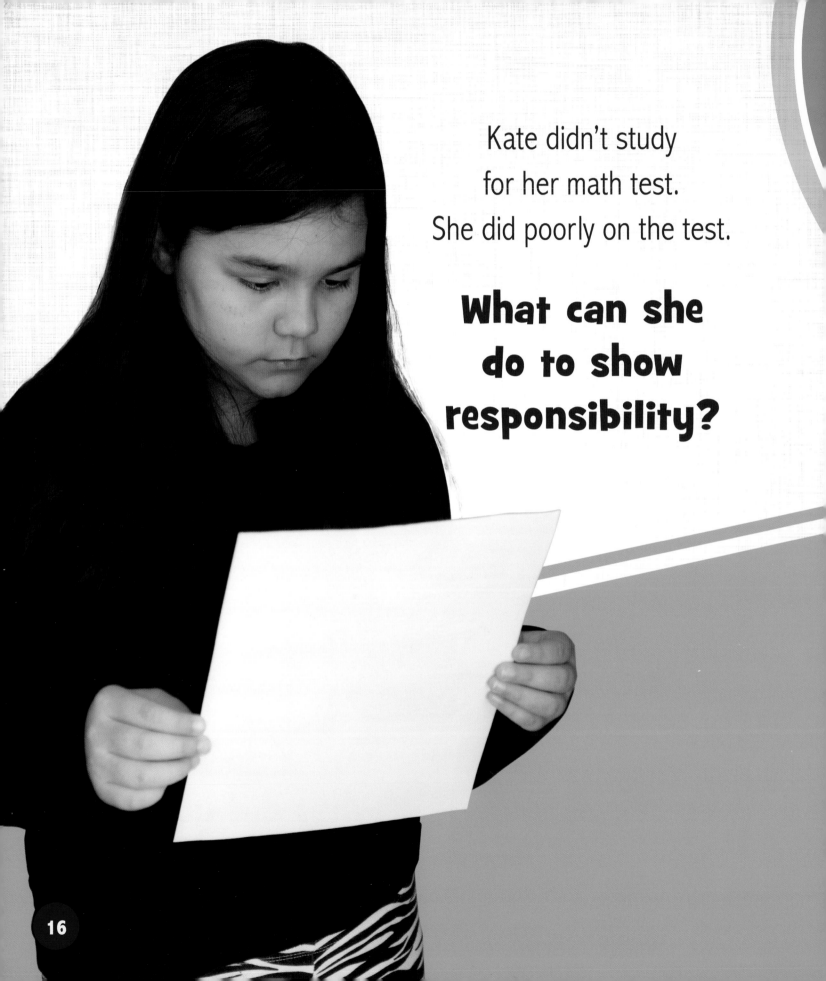

Kate didn't study
for her math test.
She did poorly on the test.

**What can she
do to show
responsibility?**

Kate doesn't make excuses.
She takes responsibility for her actions.

Can you think of a time when you took responsibility for your actions?

Colin promises to help
with chores at home.

**What can Colin do to
show he's responsible?**

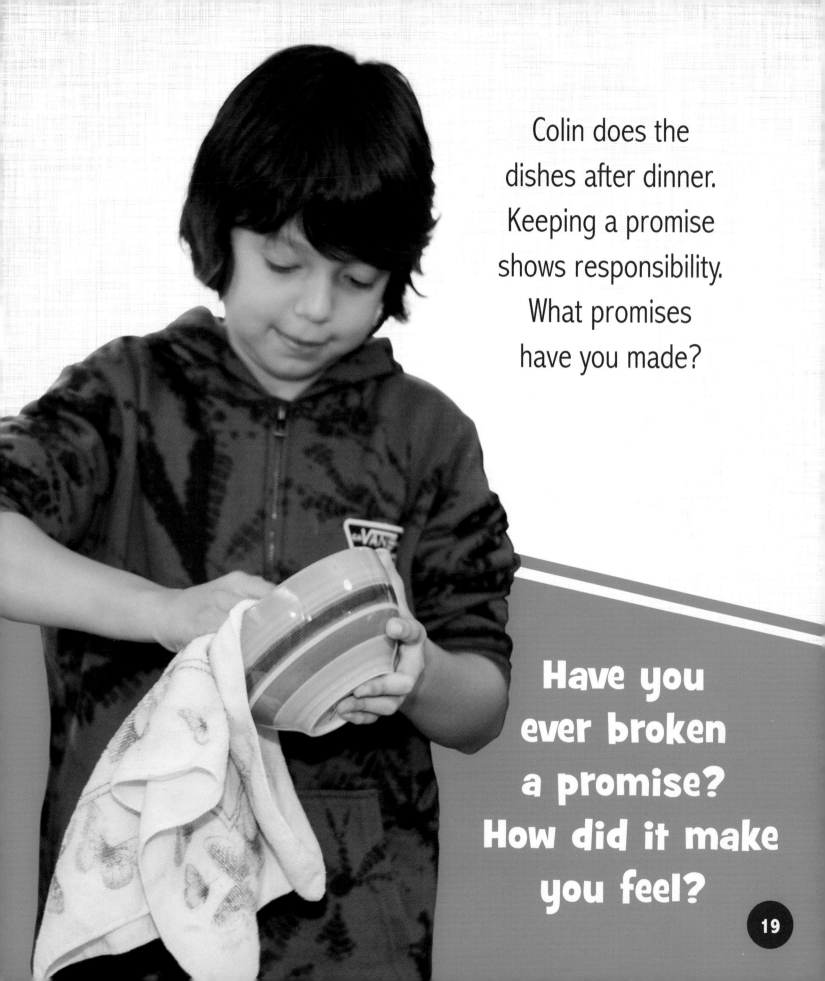

Colin does the dishes after dinner. Keeping a promise shows responsibility. What promises have you made?

Have you ever broken a promise? How did it make you feel?

19

Julia knows it's important to take care of the environment.

What should she do to show responsibility?

Julia recycles her water bottle. Doing your part to help the environment shows responsibility.

What do you do to protect the environment?

21

Eli is getting ready for bed.

What should Eli do to show he's responsible?

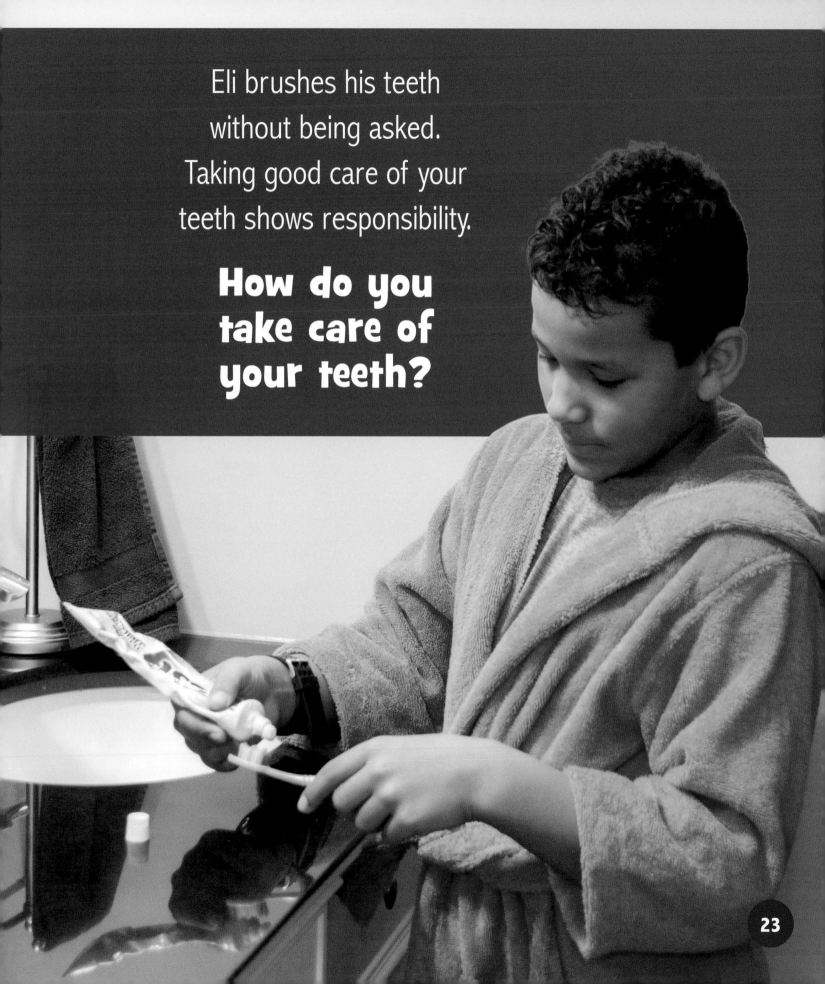

Eli brushes his teeth
without being asked.
Taking good care of your
teeth shows responsibility.

**How do you
take care of
your teeth?**

23

Olivia's library book is due today.

What should Olivia do to show she's responsible?

Olivia returns her library book.
Returning the things you
borrow shows responsibility.
Can you think of something you've borrowed?

**Did you return it when
you were supposed to?**

Mia and Logan are partners
for a science project.

**What should they do
to show responsibility?**

Mia and Logan split the work.

Doing your part shows you are responsible.

Have you ever had to share work with someone?

James is excited about going outside after lunch. He accidentally bumps the table and spills his drink.

What should James do to show responsibility?

James stays inside and cleans up the mess.
Even though the spill was an accident,
it's his responsibility to clean it up.

Have you ever had to miss out on something fun because you were being responsible?

Glossary

accidentally—without meaning to

chore—a job that has to be done regularly; washing dishes and taking out the garbage are chores

environment—all of the trees, plants, water, and dirt

excuse—a reason you give to explain a mistake or why you have done something wrong

partner—a person who works or does some other activity with another person

responsible—doing what you say you will do; people who are responsible keep promises and follow rules

Internet Sites

Use FactHound to find Internet sites related to this book:

Visit *www.facthound.com*

Just type in 9781515772019 and go.

Read More

Cook, Julia. *But It's Not My Fault!* Responsible Me! Boys Town, Neb.: Boys Town Press, 2016.

Higgins, Melissa. *I Am Responsible*. I Don't Bully. North Mankato, Minn.: Capstone Press, 2014.

Ponto, Joanna. *Being Responsible.* All About Character. New York: Enslow Publishing, 2016.

Critical Thinking Questions

1. How does Julia show responsibility toward the environment?

2. Making excuses does not show responsibility. What is an excuse? Hint: Use your glossary!

3. Can you think of a time you were responsible? What did you do?

Index

A+ Books are published by Capstone Press,
1710 Roe Crest Drive, North Mankato, Minnesota 56003
www.mycapstone.com

Library of Congress Cataloging-in-Publication Data
Cataloging-in-publication information is on file with the Library of Congress.

ISBN: 978-1-5157-7201-9 (library binding)
ISBN: 978-1-5157-7205-7 (eBook PDF)

Editorial Credits
Jaclyn Jaycox, editor; Heidi Thompson, designer; Jo Miller, media researcher;
Laura Manthe, production specialist; Marcy Morin, scheduler

Photo Credits
All photographs by Capstone Studio/Karon Dubke, except:
Shutterstock: michaeljung, 26, 27, RoyStudioEU throughout,
(background texture)

Printed in the United States of America
010374F17